MY
LITTLE
PARIS

The best kept
Parisian secrets

MY LITTLE PARIS

The best kept Parisian secrets

A translation by Catherine Taret

CHÊNE

To create a book, you need to:

**STEP OUTSIDE
YOUR HOME**

Fany Péchiodat,
Explorer and founder
of My Little Paris

FIND INSPIRATION WHERE IT AWAITS YOU

Amandine Péchiodat,
Editor and writer

Anne-Flore Brunet,
Editor and writer

**MAKE SOME SENSE
OF IT ALL**

Catherine Taret,
Book editor, writer and
translator

**TAKE IN EVERYTHING,
EVERYWHERE,
ALL THE TIME**

Kanako Kuno,
Illustrator

**KNOW EVERYTHING ABOUT
HELVETICA BOLD 12**

Mademoiselle Lilly,
Art director

Shake up this little tribe
and let them debate, argue, make up
and change their minds 54 times...

...and you will end up with a
book. Simple, non?

FOREWORD

This book would not exist if...

Fany hadn't randomly pushed the door of 39 Rue de Bretagne, and stumbled upon the best guava juice of her life.

Amandine hadn't cried her eyes out on April 3rd 2008 because she had just been laid off.

Kanako hadn't flown in from Tokyo on May 2nd 2005, with a burning desire to draw Parisian Women.

Anne-Flore hadn't been sitting in the car when Fany failed her driving license test for the 4th time.

Céline hadn't tired of financial graphics.

Catherine hadn't decided to become a writer, looking out her window on the morning of February 2nd 2010.

Mademoiselle Lilly needed more than 4 hours of sleep a night.

Toni hadn't taken up a job with an airline company in 1973.

A man wearing glasses hadn't been our own "yes you can."

Georges hadn't met Chantal at the Nogent dance on the 7th of July 1968.

Volcy hadn't left a message on Fany's machine, offering to make a book.

TO DO LIST

Things to do in Paris

√ Have dinner in a one-table restaurant
√ Send yourself an email in 10 years
√ Play Cinderella at Paris Fashion Week
√ Spice up your walls
√ Confide in a stranger over the phone
√ Lose weight, no diet
√ Plant your own vegetable patch
√ Try a fish pedicure
√ Clone your favorite clothes
√ Try being compulsive
√ Eat live noodles
√ Rent a private pool for an hour
√ Furnish your home like a movie set
√ Have one orgasm a week
√ Explore Paris's secret outlet stores
√ Let special agents rescue you from stress
√ Have a Chinese massage at home
√ Be a guinea pig for a future three-star chef
√ Become a member of the Mile High Club
√ Say merci
√ Eat your pizza with truffles on top
√ Enjoy an acrobatic Japanese meal
√ Be a star in your own home
√ Thread your eyebrows
√ Pretend you are a connoisseur
√ Have your panties delivered
√ Lose it over an Italian cheese

√ Try the killer secret detail
√ Join in on the Dead Poet's Society
√ Rummage around for deco objects
√ Wear a hat that's made just for you
√ Learn Dirty Dancing
√ Sip a cocktail in a dreamy hideaway
√ Have a cocktail named after you
√ Rediscover forgotten veggies
√ (Almost) wear couture
√ Don't drink and email
√ Put yourself in good hands
√ Accept a non-marriage proposal
√ Turn your kids into little Picassos
√ Catch a concert in 7th heaven
√ Indulge in the best ham in the world
√ Dress like a VIP
√ Make a deal with the granny gang
√ Brunch to the tune of the four seasons
√ Turn your home into a (coffee-table) book
√ Attend a crazy trial
√ Make a stop at the chignon bar
√ Attend a clandestine dinner
√ Fight the Sunday night blues
√ Have fresh produce delivered to your home
√ Laugh out loud
√ Change your lingerie, change your life
√ Have lunch at the market

CHALLENGES

In a Parisian rut?
Try any of these simple remedies.

WALK DOWN AVENUE MONTAIGNE WEARING NOTHING BUT YOUR TRENCH

TRADE APARTMENTS WITH ANOTHER PARISIAN JUST FOR A WEEKEND

GO UP TO THE 3RD FLOOR WITH PAUL, THE MYSTERIOUS "ELEVATOR MAN," AT THE MARCHÉ SAINT-PIERRE

JUMP INTO A CAB AND SAY: "FOLLOW THAT CAR!"

HAVE A GLASS OF CHAMPAGNE, BY YOURSELF, AT THE BAR OF A 5-STAR HOTEL

TRAVEL THE METRO IN THE DRIVER'S CAB

SPEND AN ENTIRE EVENING SPEAKING ONLY IN CLICHÉS

GO TO THE "WHITE DINNER" DRESSED IN BLACK

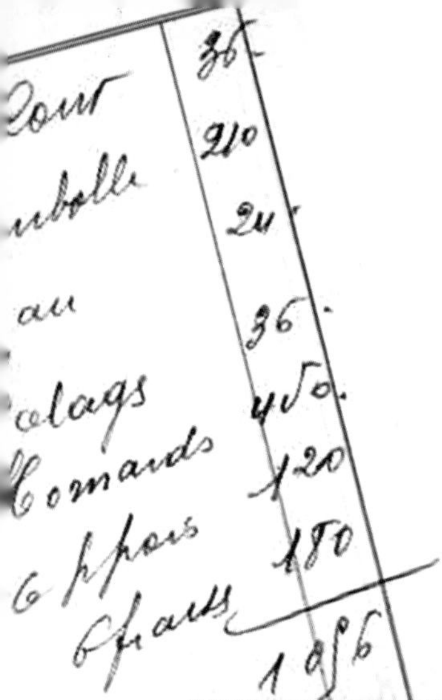

Pour   36—
            210
            24
au   36.
clags   450.
Comands   120
6 h pois   180
Crans
            1056

la tête dans les olives

Have dinner in a one-table restaurant

Forget Jacques, he's kinda boring. And Brigitte? Too chatty.

You are going to have to be very fussy when you make up your guest list of just four lucky friends to invite to Cedric Casanova's table. The proud Sicilian owner of Paris' finest olive oil joint, La Tête dans les Olives, is hosting very private dinners.

Kanako

At night, Cédric's tiny boutique turns into the most intimate restaurant in the city, and you may book the one and only table for 5 people. Once the evening starts, your highly selective committee will go through the most deliciously inventive Italian meal starting, no surprise, by an olive oil tasting. Then, you will be amazed by the salted ricotta beets and sweet-and-sour pumpkin from Palerma. Next thing you know you are discovering the delicate tuna bresaola carpaccio. Please stay calm when the huge olives and the freshest capers appear.

It's like a fantasy. So really, the tough part is choosing your dream team.

One table in the shop "La Tête dans les Olives."
Price for 5 people: starting from €30 per person.
The menu varies with deliveries from Sicily.
La Tête dans les Olives
2 rue Sainte-Marthe, Paris 10th.
Metro Goncourt.
For reservations call +33 (0)9 51 31 33 34 or +33 (0)6 73 75 74 81 from 9am to 7pm.
Open daily for lunch and dinner.

15

Dear FutureMe,

Don't ask Brandon out. Ever!

WRITTEN: December 20, 2005
SENT: December 20, 2006

Arriving at Finisterra having walked there from Le Puy… I should have
turned left and gone to Portugal, not right and returned to Scotland … I
have never felt so well, in both mind and body, my life was never filled
with so much potential …

- - - - - - - - - -

Sleeping beside my camp fire in the Namibian bush.

WRITTEN: December 31, 2005
SENT: December 31, 2006

I guess you have kids as well. Be fair to them. Try and
mind. Don't do anything they wouldn't want. Althou
the best advice. °imagines what life would be like if N

Anyway, I hope you have a wonderful birthday, and I
last 25 years to good use.

Love,
PastMe

WRITTEN: February 20, 2006
SENDING: November 06, 2031

r FutureMe,

utureMe,
e I am still with David, because I am going to
iis name tattooed today. So if I'm not, I'll prob-
y be laughing when I read this.

RITTEN: February 18, 2006
ENT: April 01, 2007

Dear FutureMe,
Don't ask Brandon out. Ever!
WRITTEN: December 20, 2005
SENT: December 20, 2006

Needless to say, the very second I realised that I had attained this comfortable state I set about getting rid of it all.

- - - - - - - - - -

Aegean, night, fishing boats: I remember sitting on the shore of Naxos
Island, a warm night and a full belly, out at sea I watched the distant
soundless lights of fishing boats moving to and fro …

- - - - - - - - - -

Paris, a night of wild sex with two beautiful women. Nuff said …

- - - - - - - - - -

Send yourself an email in 10 years

"Dear FutureMe.
When I open this email 10 years from now, I hope I am
a successful writer, living in a loft. I also hope I'm still
with Matthieu because I had his name tattooed on my
arm today."

Do you have a promise to make, a feeling you wish to remember, a goal to set? Then send yourself an email with www.FutureMe.com and pick the date you'd like to receive it, maybe in a few months or a few years. *Rendezvous* in the future.

www.futureme.org

date :
remarques :

Play Cinderella
at Paris Fashion Week

Fashion Week is a marathon. To make it to the final run(way), you need two essentials: the right dose of fluids (champagne) and the right footwear (15 cm Louboutin heels).

If your shoes give up on you from all the standing and screening and dancing, don't wait for some Prince Charming to offer you a stiletto. Race to "Minuit moins 7" (seven minutes till midnight). This shoe-repairer is the only one in the glamour world who can replace authentic red Christian Louboutin soles. Or make a cocktail stain magically disappear from your pumps, replace a heel, enlarge a boot or provide nourishing cream for any color leather.

It can be pricey but it's the price to pay for perfection. And you might get some wise advice thrown in, such as: "Walk 10 minutes every day with wet socks in your shoes if you want them to feel like slippers." Smart.

Minuit moins 7
10, Galerie Véro-Dodat, Paris 1st.
Metro Louvre–Rivoli.
Tel: +33 (0)1 42 21 15 47.
For all brands of shoes.
It takes one week and €94 to replace the red soles.

FRIENDSHIP

We all have a friend who is…

ON A DIET *"Damn that Nutella!"*	**NEVER THERE** ....
ALWAYS SHOWING OFF	**THE OWNER OF A HOUSE IN NORMANDY** ....
FREE TO SPEND SUNDAY NIGHTS WITH YOU *"Do you think he's gonna call?"*	**ALWAYS ON THE PHONE** *"Hang on, I have another call."* ....
OBSESSED Jean-Yves: 15/20	**NEVER STRESSED** *"Keep cool, chérie."* ....

FED UP WITH PARIS *"Tomorrow, I'm out of here!"*	 **A DRAG** *"I've lost my keys, can I stay at your place?"* ....
 **OVERBOOKED** *"I have an opening on April 16th, from 10 to 10.30pm."*	 **NEVER TURNED AWAY AT THE BARON CLUB** ....
 **ALWAYS READY TO PARTY**	**STILL SINGLE** *"Women don't know what they want…"* ....
A WANNABE WRITER *"I am starting tomorrow…"*	 **NOT SURE ABOUT MUCH** *"Oui… but non…"* ....

Spice up your walls

You have just moved into a new Parisian apartment and you're dying to make it look like an artist's hideaway. But unfortunately it's just too tiny. Forget about pushing back the walls. Instead create an illusion.

The boutique "The Collection," located in the Marais, offers crafty decorators a great selection of creative wall decor material: from delirious stickers to photo wallpaper. You will only need a few minutes and a bit of concentration to spice up that boring blank space in the salon with a beautiful and nonetheless imaginary bookcase or create the illusion of a vintage lamp on your end table.

The Collection
33 rue de Poitou, Paris 3rd.
Metro Filles du Calvaire.
Tel: +33 (0)1 42 77 04 20.
www.thecollection.fr

Kanako

Confide in a stranger over the phone

"My name is Sophie Calle. You are standing in my phone booth. I alone know the number and I dial it from time to time, always hoping that somebody will pick up."

These lines are engraved on the wall of a phone booth, perched on the Garigliano Bridge. Sophie Calle, the French thought-provoking artist, thought of it while inspired by another famous phone booth, planted in the middle of the desert. So at any moment, she might dial the number and a total (not to mention astonished) stranger might pick up. They could very well end up chitchatting for a few seconds or conversing for hours. It's what they call *destinée*.

Sophie Calle's Phone booth
Under the flower-shaped sculpture on the Garigliano Bridge, Paris 15th. Metro Balard.

Lose weight, no diet

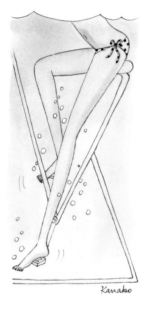

Kanako

Pedal in a pool

On the surface, everything appears normal. You are simply splashing around in a cozy urban pool. But under the water, your legs are slaving away, pedaling their way out of winter cellulite. This is no torture device. It's aqua biking.

Put on your bikini, enter the pool, choose one of the bikes anchored to the bottom and start pedaling. All that cycling under water, for at least 45 minutes, massages your body and erases cellulite much more efficiently than any other method. The stimulating music and your aqua-bike teacher help you focus on the exercise and forget about your escape plan.

Aquabiking
€30 for a 45-minute class; a towel will be lent to you.
€25 for a class if you have a 10-class subscription.

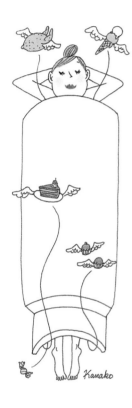

Kanako

Melt while dozing off

That was then: a few centuries ago in Japan, people used to bury themselves in hot sand to eliminate toxins from their body.

This is now: you lay naked in the Iyashi Dôme, a sort of soft, cozy tunnel, where heat enters gently. Don't worry. Your head stays outside of course, so you can breathe the air in the room. Close your eyes and doze off for 30 minutes, while your body cleanses itself and expels toxins and calories.

La Maison Popincourt
4 cité Popincourt, Paris 11th.
Metro Saint-Ambroise.
Tel: +33 (0)1 43 38 96 84.

Iyashi Dôme
30-minute session: €45.

"I love the things I will never understand."

Amélie Nothomb

Plant your own vegetable patch

Every Parisian's secret fantasy: *"Someday, I will leave the city and buy a house in the countryside, breed goats and grow tomatoes in my own garden."*

We're still looking for the goat; as for the plot, consider it done. Shared vegetable gardens have been blooming all over Paris, and surely there is one just waiting to help you fulfill your farmer's dream: someplace to nurture your flowers and plant your cabbages, maybe just a few blocks down your street.

All you need to do is contact the nonprofit organization in charge of your targeted patch and then become a member. You'll be invited to get involved in the social life of your gardening community: collective soups, improvised picnics, *cafés au jardin... la belle vie!*

www.jardinons-ensemble.org

Serre aux Légumes

Un P'tit Bol d'Air

Les Jardins Passagers

Jardins du Ruisseau

Eco Box

Rue du Maroc

La Framboisine

Jardin de Perlimpinpin

18e

Le Bois Dormoy

Charmante Petite Campagne Urbaine

Le Trèfle d'Éole

Jardin d'Léon

Jardin Crimée-Thionville

17e

Jardin des 2 Nèthes

19e

Jardin des Petits Passages

L'îlot Lilas

Jardin Victor Schoelcher

Église Saint-Serge

Square Alexandre Luquet

9e

Jardin du passage Hébrard

Jardin Fessart

10e

Leroy 5ème

8e

Le Poireau Agile

Jardin de la Butte Bergeyre

Jardin des Soupirs

Rue Henri Duvernois

Jardin aux Habitants

2e

Le Centre de la Terre

16e

3e

1er

Potager des Oiseaux

11e

Papilles et Papillons

Le 56

7e

1001 Feuilles

Pouce on plante

Jardins du Béton Saint-Blaise

4e

Jardin Nomade

20e

Le Jardin sur le Toit

6e

Jardin partagé de la Folie Titon

Les Haies Partagées

Jardin partagé Fleurs de Bitume

5e

Aligresse

Le Jardin du 12e

Jardin partagé des Périchaux

15e

Jardin partagé du square du Chanoine Viollet

Jardins familiaux du bd de l'Hôpital

12e

Jardin Bel-Air

Jardin de Falbala

Jardin Jean Genet

Le Lapin Ouvrier

Jardin partagé du square Auguste-Renoir

14e

Jardin de l'Aqueduc

13e

Jardin partagé de la rue de Coulmiers

Les Jardins Malins

Jardin partagé des Mots et Merveilles

Jardin partagé de la Poterne des Peupliers

Try
A fish pedicure

Malaysia, China, Japan... The fish doctors have swum their way through Asia, fulfilling their curious calling: exfoliating and massaging people's feet. They are now swirling around in Paris.

The fish therapy center is just a stone's throw away from the Pantheon, in the heart of the Latin Quarter. Who would guess that tiny aquatic fauna hides inside this old half-timbered house? Take a seat and hold still as an aquarium suddenly appears from the ground. Plunge your feet into the water and try not to giggle as tiny fish start exfoliating your skin. The Garra rufa (called fish doctors because of their therapeutic virtues) ask only to paddle their way around your toes, polish off the dead skin and soften your feet. Once they are done, you feel like you've had a fabulous massage and a neat pedicure. Don't try it with your goldfish! Not just any fish can call itself a fish doctor!

Rufa Fish Spa
3 rue des Fossés Saint-Jacques, Paris 5th.
RER Luxembourg.
Tel. +33 (0)1 43 29 41 36.

Kanako

Find the perfect apartment in Paris

Facing the Opéra
To have a ringside seat

Overlooking a fire station
For the Sunday morning warm-up

Above the Pâtisserie des Rêves
To stock up on goodies at any hour

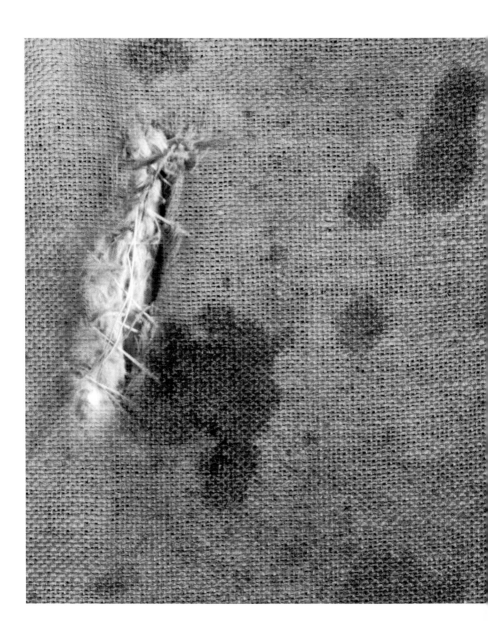

Clone
your favorite clothes

It's over. It took you years to find the perfect ones, the ones that brought out the best in you: beauty, confidence. You'll never get over them. You'll never be able to replace them.

Your favorite black pants, your fetish stilettos. Worn out. Don't do anything desperate. In Paris, a resurrection of romance is always possible. Or at least a good copy.

www.jeveuxlememe.fr
The creators of the website (which means "I want the same.com") offer to borrow your favorite piece of clothing and clone it back to reality.
If you're okay with their price, they'll have it delivered to your place in Paris.

Pants from €60, shirts from €40, a dress from €50.
www.jeveuxlememe.fr

La Boutique Sentimentale
This shoe repairer creates a copy of your beloved shoes in any color or material.

14 rue du Roi de Sicile, Paris 4th.
Metro Saint-Paul.
Tel: +33 (0)1 42 78 84 04.
Open Tuesday to Sunday 2pm to 7pm.

Kanako

"Everything in your closet
should have an expiration date on it
the way milk and bread and magazines
and newspapers do."

Andy Warhol

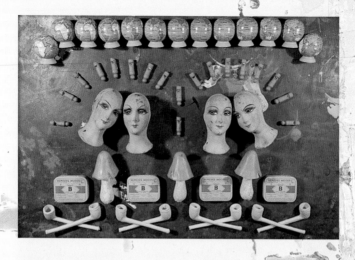

Try being compulsive

Parisian women live to collect. Chanel, cocktail party invitations, glamorous souvenirs and men are their obvious passions. But you'd be surprised as to what else they choose to hunt for and hoard.

Tombées du Camion, (literally "fallen off the truck") is a secret collector's paradise offering compulsive accumulators loads of unusual, weird or forgotten objects. What exactly can you find here? An abundance of the smallest retro treasures that can take you for a nostalgic ride through your past and end up livening up your living room. Let's see what you've found... The exact copy of your 7th grade planet-shaped pencil sharpener, wooden printer's letters to decorate your mantelpiece, a bunch of those vintage doll eyeballs, a piece or two of that funky plastic jewelry and some old postcards. And you thought you were a compulsive shopper.

Kanako

Tombées du Camion
17 rue Joseph de Maistre, Paris 18th.
Metro Blanche.
Open Tuesday to Friday 1pm to 8pm
and Saturday and Sunday 11am to 8pm.

EAT
live noodles

Rue du Faubourg Montmartre is quite a busy street. Except at number 46. At this precise spot, rushers-by stop and rub elbows on the sidewalk, fascinated by the vision of a Chinese woman, working in a shop window. She's stretching and rolling something, as though she were spinning cotton thread, but actually, she's making fresh pasta.

Number 46 is an Asian restaurant, called *Les Pâtes Vivantes* (literally "Live Pasta"). After a *mise en bouche* of brisk tempura, order a bowl of noodles à la sauce Chajiang, and let the show begin. Soon the tender beef, crispy soy, exuberant mustard leaves and vigorous ginger start wriggling in your mouth. Hold on tight to your chopsticks to capture the noodles, which are so long and fresh that they seem to dance in your plate as if they were alive! We should warn you that, unless you have spent years in China, there is little chance you'll walk out of this canteen with your dignity and a clean shirt. Not allowed for first dates, but highly recommended for healthy appetites.

Les Pâtes Vivantes
46 rue du Faubourg Montmartre, Paris 9th.
Metro Le Peletier.
Tel: +33 (0)1 45 23 10 21.

The deepest Parisian fears

Missing the last metro

—

Not finding a table on the terrace of the bar du Marché

—

Wearing the same Zara top as your colleague

—

Bumping into your ex, when walking out of the gym, sweating

—

Being home alone on a Saturday night

—

Moving to the suburbs

—

Getting mobbed by a pigeon

—

Not finding a parking spot for your Velib bike

—

Realizing that your neighbor might actually
be having a sexual life

—

Being mistaken for a *provinciale* (non-Parisian)

—

RENT
A PRIVATE POOL FOR AN HOUR

Once Oscar Wilde's haven, L'Hôtel now appeals to the likes of Johnny Depp and Vanessa Paradis. On Rue des Beaux-Arts, it is no less than a legendary address. And you can humbly play your role in its story.

Start by sinking into a deep velvet chair softened by the dim lighting of the lounge. Order the cocktail *de la maison* (champagne, violet and lime) and enjoy the moment. But that's hardly all The Hotel has to offer. Under the medieval arches, hidden behind a heavy velvet curtain lies a mysterious underground swimming pool. This pool can be privatized for a whole hour, for a relaxing swim by yourself or a romantic plunge with a very special someone. Oscar Wilde wrote that "the only way to get rid of a temptation is to yield to it." Maybe that's where Oscar Wilde wrote that "the only way to get rid of a temptation is to yield to it."

"Treat and Eat" for 2 – privatized pool + massage (30 min) + lunch: €130 per person.
"Treat and Eat" for 1 – privatized pool + massage (1 hour) + lunch: €190 per person.
Tuesday to Saturday, lunch only.

L'Hôtel
13 rue des Beaux-Arts, Paris 6th.
Metro Saint-Germain-des-Prés.
www.l-hotel.com

47

Furnish your Home like a movie set

This is the secret place where stylists, photographers and filmmakers shop to create an authentic movie set. It's also a favorite destination for design addicts and collectors hunting for bargain treasures.

Walking into the XXO warehouse is like stepping into another time zone, where movie sets and extravagant pieces of furniture mix and match in a 2000-square-meter loft.

First there's the whole cast of Plexiglas chairs adorned with a geisha image and designed by Philippe Starck, which seated most of the jet set at Kong restaurant in Paris (you might have caught a glimpse of them in "Sex in the City's" last episode). Then there's an electric blue chair with unmistakable lines, spotted in last month's trendy magazine *Ideat*.

A nice change from your afternoon at Ikea.

Kanako

XXO
78 rue de la Fraternité, 93 230 Romainville.
Tel: +33 (0)1 48 18 08 88.
www.xxo.com
Open Monday to Friday 9am to 6pm
and every first Saturday of the month.
How to get there: Take metro line 11 to Mairie des Lilas, then hop on bus 105 and bus 129. Approximately 45 min from Châtelet metro station.

HAVE ONE ORGASM PER WEEK

Do you feel you're in a rut in your cooking routine? Spice it up with this very special recipe for Fondant au Chocolat.

The secret? A luscious blend of chocolate, pepper and ginger for two-stage pleasure: the ginger arouses your desire and excites your taste buds, while the pepper sets off an internal fire. You can't help asking for more.

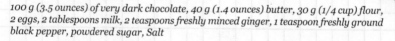

Here is the fatally attractive recipe (for two):

100 g (3.5 ounces) of very dark chocolate, 40 g (1.4 ounces) butter, 30 g (1/4 cup) flour, 2 eggs, 2 tablespoons milk, 2 teaspoons freshly minced ginger, 1 teaspoon freshly ground black pepper, powdered sugar, Salt

Preheat oven to 220°C. Butter and sugar two individual ramekins and save them in the fridge. Cut the chocolate into squares. Keep 8 pieces on the side. In a small pan, melt the butter and all the chocolate except for the 8 pieces. Let sit.

Separate the egg whites from the yolks. Whip the egg whites in a mixer until light and fluffy.

Mix the egg yolks with 2 teaspoons sugar until they whiten. Add the milk, the flour, a pinch of salt and the melted chocolate. Then delicately blend in the whipped egg whites.

In another small pan, heat ¾ cup of water, the ginger, pepper and a tablespoon of sugar until you obtain a syrup. Let the syrup cool. Once the syrup has cooled down, add the 8 remaining pieces of chocolate and stir until the mixture is smooth. If needed, you can put the pan back on the fire to melt the chocolate completely. Be careful not to add the chocolate to the hot syrup... it will burn!

Distribute half the chocolate mix into the ramekins. Then delicately pour the spice syrup so that it is at the center of the ramekins, and then top it off with the rest of the chocolate mix.

Cook for 10 minutes until the surface of the cakes starts cracking. Eat warm.

This recipe is taken from the book:
"480 pages de douceurs dans un monde de brutes"
Chez Tana Editions, Collection Mon grain de sel ©*Raphaële Vidaling*

Explore Paris's
SECRET OUTLETS STORES

If you're thinking about investing in Paris, we suggest you put your money in the city's greatest asset: fashion.

Our best addresses for outlet stores in the city:

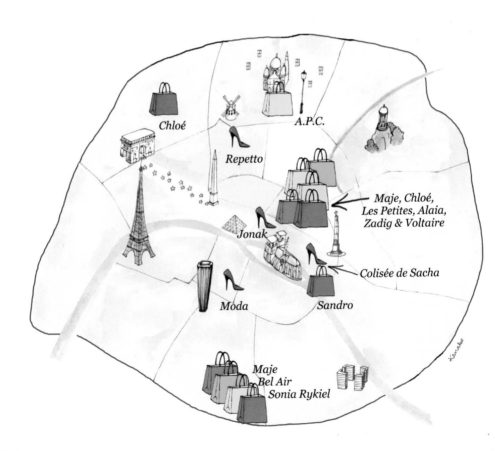

Chloé

A.P.C.

Repetto

Maje, Chloé,
Les Petites, Alaia,
Zadig & Voltaire

Jonak

Colisée de Sacha

Moda

Sandro

Maje
Bel Air
Sonia Rykiel

Sandro outlet
26 rue de Sévigné, 4th

Chloé outlet
8 rue Jean-Pierre Timbaud, 11th

Maje outlet
- 44 avenue du Général Leclerc, 14th
- 92 rue des Martyrs, 18th

Repetto outlet
24 rue de Châteaudun, 9th

Jonak outlet
44 boulevard Sébastopol, 3rd

**Modaoutlet
(high-end designer shoes)**
45 rue Saint-Placide, 6th

Zadig et Voltaire outlet
22 rue du Bourg Tibourg, 4th

APC outlet
20 rue André Del Sarte, 18th

Bel Air outlet
36 avenue du Général Leclerc, 14th

Alaïa outlet
18 rue de la Verrerie, 9th

Sonia Rykiel outlet
64 rue d'Alésia, 14th

Colisée de Sacha outlet
59 rue Beaubourg, 4th

Les Petites outlet
11 rue de Marseille, 10th

Let special agents rescue you from stress

New Yorkers have free hugs. Parisians get free massages, given by zealous Zen-enforcement officers. Is it a new government policy? Not really. They are members of a nonprofit group called "La Décontraction à la Française" (literally "Relaxing the French Way") who practice street massage for the sole pleasure of Parisians.

They are waiting for you on the little Place de la Contrescarpe, with their magic touch hands and inviting smiles, ready to hand out a free and relaxing back rub. Sit. Close your eyes. Let the sound of soft gypsy music wash away your thoughts. Your head, your arms, your hands, your back, your entire body is softly kneaded and emptied of any remaining stress. Feeling better?

« La Décontraction à la française »
Nonprofit organization
Place de la Contrescarpe,
6 rue Blainville, Paris 5th.
Metro Place Monge.
Tel: +33 (0)6 63 91 86 35
For more information, please write to
decontraction.france@gmail.com
Starting at 6pm, every sunny day,
from early May to end of September.

HAVE A CHINESE MASSAGE AT HOME

Too flabby, too expensive, too chatty. We scoured the entire 13th *arrondissement* in search of the best Chinese masseur. And then we finally got lucky.

The Liu family, a man and a woman, totally bewitched our feet! This couple can come to your home and treat your feet to one hour of pure traditional Chinese bliss for only €40.

Ding dong: the duo enters the apartment and once they have transformed your place into a massage salon, the Chinese ritual may begin. While your feet are relaxing in a bath of roses, Liu massages your head, back and arms. Then they focus on "your body's second heart," your feet. Liu rubs, kneads, and molds every inch of each foot and you can feel the benefits spread through your whole body.

The hour is over, Liu disappears and you just know you've experienced pure heaven.

Liu Massage
Foot massage at home in Paris, 7 days a week, from 9am to 11pm.
Make an appointment by phone: +33 (0)6 10 19 95 27 then confirm your address by mail: massageliu@hotmail.com
Price: €40 an hour in Paris; €10 extra for the suburbs (Neuilly-sur-Seine and Levallois).

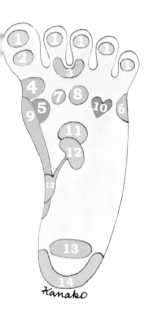

Kanako

1. soothes your thoughts
2. sets your mind to rest
3. relaxes your eyes
4. dilutes your stress
5. drains off your stress
6. dissolves the knots in your shoulders
7. calms down your breathing
8. balances your circulation
9. relaxes your back
10. harmonizes your heart rhythm
11. contributes to the wellbeing of your body and mind
12. calms your stomach
13. boosts your energy
14. stimulates your circulation

"If you play by the rules,
you miss all the fun."

Katherine Hepburn

BE A GUINEA PIG
FOR A FUTURE THREE-STAR CHEF

The wine steward is a bit clumsy as he fills your glass and the maître d' can't remember the name of the appetizer *du jour*. In any other restaurant, we would be ruthless. But in this one, we're delighted. That's what you get when you treat yourself to a luxurious meal in a restaurant school....and for a tiny price to boot!

Vatel is a training institute for future gourmet chefs. While you're busy feasting on a three-course meal, they are silently sweating because they know their teacher is around, scrutinizing their every move. These people are serious about food and service: the selection of refined seasonal dishes is worthy of a starred restaurant, and the check is only €33. The best part of the meal is when a blushing junior pastry chef comes to your table and presents you with his patisseries. You feel like applauding.

Kanako

Institut Vatel
122 rue Nollet, 17th.
Metro Brochant.
Open Monday to Friday.
Make a reservation by calling +33 (0)1 42 26 26 60.
Lunch and dinner formulas at €33
(appetizer, main course, cheese and dessert).
Lunch special for €21 (main course and dessert).

Become a member
of the Mile High Club

"I'm worried about Martine, she just hasn't been her-self since she flew back from New York."
Quite normal, how could anyone understand Martine anymore? Since that red-eye flight she took, she's become a member of the most exclusive club in the world: the club of those who've done it on a plane.

Joining the Mile High Club is not easy. For one thing, you need to get an engine to fly you over the minimum one-mile altitude required by the rules. Then you need to find yourself a reliable partner willing to help you hit the cabin ceiling. Finally, you need a good strategy. Choose a seat near the aisle, take note of the flight attendant's whereabouts, avoid the rush hour lineup at the lavatories and be ready for action as soon as the lights go off. Once you've reached dry land, the detailed story of this initiation rite will open the doors to this restricted order. You will shortly receive an official membership card.

We hope you have a pleasant flight.

www.milehighclub.com
Mile High Club: the club of those who've "done it" in an airplane

CARTE D'ADHÉRENT
MILE HIGH CLUB

N° ....1635..378983

Nom et Prénom : ..Raphaëlle..Raymond

Adresse :.127..rue..de..l'Université
          75006 Paris

Date d'adhésion :..12..06..2004....

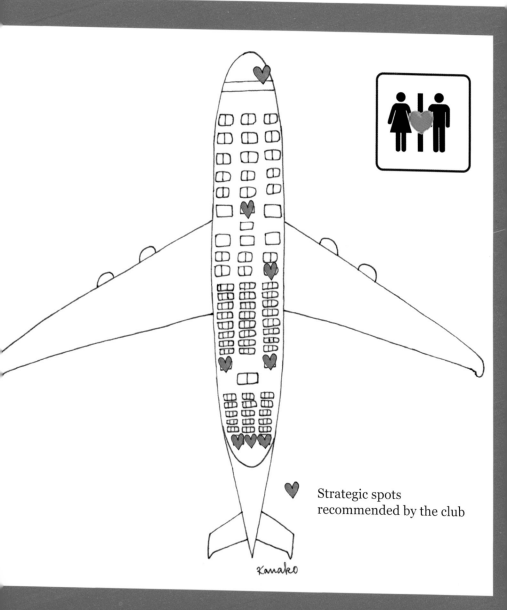

Strategic spots
recommended by the club

SAY MERCI

I wish *(my boyfriend would offer me flowers more often)*
You want *(the new Louboutins)*...
He requested *(a seat near the window)*...
There are some words that we conjugate in every possible
way. And others that we tend to forget...."Thank you" for
example. It's a common expression, for a not-so-common
attitude.

A temple to gratitude lies in the heart of Paris, in the Marais. Bernard and Marie-France Cohen, founders of Bon-
point, have created a charity concept store to celebrate the
many gifts that life has given them and share their great
success with less fortunate people. Naturally, the store is
called Merci. It's located in a majestic, sun-lit loft where
you can browse from room to room just like in a real house.
Shop for designer clothes, buy a tiny bunch of roses at the
flower shop, cuddle up on a sofa in the book corner and sip
a lemonade. You're not going to believe this, but you'll be
raising money! The profits the store makes on your pur-
chases are donated to charities.

Don't you already feel better?

Merci
111 Boulevard Beaumarchais, Paris 3rd.
Metro Saint-Sébastien–Froissart.
Tel: +33 (0)1 42 77 00 33.
Open Monday to Saturday 10am to 8pm.

HAVE YOUR PIZZA WITH TRUFFLES ON TOP

Kanako

Truffle: it's a precious black diamond that all too rarely delights our taste buds. It's the almost invisible, yet unmistakable star of any dish it is part of, whether it's pasta, an omelet or now even pizza.

Pizza *à la truffe* is the specialty of Al Taglio, one of the best pizza places in the city. The finest selection of ingredients, fresh from Italy, are combined with a light, crispy dough. The pizza is served as in Rome: by weight.

If you're not in an exclusively truffle mood, you can mix and match your pizza order, choosing a 200g truffle cream pizza, plus a 100g pancetta and pumpkin cream pizza plus a 150g buffala and basil pizza.

This pizza can also be delivered straight to your doorstep, if you ever feel like impressing your blasé friends. Or eating an extra 100g.

Al Taglio
Pizza by weight and by slice.
28 rue Neuve Popincourt, Paris 11th.
Metro Parmentier.
Tel: +33 (0)1 43 38 12 00.
Open Tuesday to Thursday, noon to 11 pm,
Friday and Saturday noon to midnight.
Deliveries inside Paris for a minimum extra large pan
serving 8 to 10 people: starting at €30 (pizza Margherita)
to €50 (potato and truffle pizza).
Orders have to be placed at least 24 hours in advance.

Enjoy
AN ACROBATIC JAPANESE MEAL

Here your favorite veggies put on a show. They parade around the tin hot plate stage and they somersault a few times before landing graciously in your mouth. You're sitting at the Comptoir Nippon and you are attending the Teppanyaki show.

In this Japanese tradition, the cooks nimbly juggle with the prawns, chisel the veggies swiftly and play the maracas with the pepper grinders. If you concentrate and open your mouth at the right time, you will catch the tofu crêpe as it flies in your direction. The culinary spectacle is not only spellbinding, but your taste buds will also get a splash. Have a taste of the spring rolls with shiitake and foie gras, a bite of the sautéed spinach à la peanuts, and a dash of the lobster rolls stuffed with sea urchin.

Recommended for perking up a business meal or loosening up a first date.

Kanako

Au Comptoir Nippon
3 avenue du Maine, Paris 15th.
Tel: +33 (0)1 45 48 22 32.
Metro Montparnasse.
Formulas start at €26.50.
As you book your table, please indicate your preference:
do you wish to receive your food in your plate—or in your mouth!

Be a star
in your own Home

"Paris would not be Paris, without the Parisiennes." In their honor, a young 21st century Doisneau has immortalized them on glossy paper.

Baudouin, a famous photographer for ELLE magazine, is working on a book on Parisian women, which will be called quite simply: *Je suis une Parisienne* (I am a Parisienne). For that matter, he is looking to shoot 100 Parisian gals in their Parisian apartments. And you're invited to the casting, whether you've been living in the city for months, years or your whole life. What Baudouin is looking for, is that mysterious aura that characterizes the Parisiennes. This "je ne sais quoi" that could make you an icon in a fine coffee-table book. If you feel like having your photo taken, languishing on your bed, proudly standing in front of your vinyl record collection, or just lounging in your good old leather chair, send a photo of your most fabulous self and your enchanting home to contact@baudouin.fr. Bonne chance!

www.baudouin.fr
Look for the page entitled "I'm a Parisian lady."

THREAd
yOUR EyEbROWS

Choose your eyebrow style

Curved
à la Sienna Miller

Very curved
à la Marlene Dietrich

Angular
à la Angelina Jolie

Circumflex
à la Marilyn Monroe

Softly angular
à la Aishwarya Kai

They may well dance to the tune of those kitsch choreographies while wearing flashy saris, but Bollywood actresses need only a seductive glance to conquer the hero and the audience as well. What's their secret? Well for starters, carefully designed eyebrows, or precisely, the perfect arch.

Threading is an ancient Indian technique, where the tiny eyebrow hair is caught between two cotton threads that slide to uproot it. This method enables the tracing to be much more precise than with waxing. The beauticians at the Indian beauty center are expert and reliable trimmers and they draw an impeccable line, adapted to the shape of your eyebrow. It takes 5 minutes and costs €7. We should warn you that the first time is a bit painful, but the feeling is as great as getting a new (good) haircut: your eyes are beautified, your face lightens up and your features appear thinner. Stunning.

Indian Beauty Center
27/33 rue Philippe de Girard, Paris 10th.
Metro Gare du Nord.
Tel: +33 (0)1 46 07 44 67.
Open Tuesday to Saturday 10.30am to 8pm
and Sunday 11am to 7.30pm.
No appointment.

Kanako

Pretend
YOU ARE A CONNOISSEUR

Eating Thai noodles with a fork? Too easy. Sweetening espresso or adding vinegar to oysters? Blasphemous. Forget make-believe restaurants and choose the cuisine of the connoisseurs, those who will not be fooled; those who know how to pick an authentic joint over some vain fashionable kitchen; those who are not afraid to indulge in a dish that will put their taste buds on fire.

If you feel like wandering off the beaten track on a metro ticket, try any of these 6 no-fuss spots and plant your chopsticks into some of the best dishes in the world.

Did you enjoy it? Say thank you...
In Korean: *kam sah hamnida*
In Hindi: *dhanyavad*
In Thai: *kop khun kha* for a woman
kop khun krap for a man
In Vietnamese: *cam On*
In Japanese: *Arigatô*

**Learn the art of eating
a bibimbap**
Bibimbap
32 boulevard de l'Hôpital,
Paris 5th.
Metro Gare d'Austerlitz or
Saint-Marcel.
Tel: +33 (0)1 43 31 27 42.

Drink the best lassi in the city
Le Paris-Féni
15 bis rue Ternaux, Paris 11th.
Metro Parmentier.
Tel: +33 (0)1 48 05 08 85

**Eat *à la thaï,*
sitting on a cushion**
Le Krung Thep
93 rue Julien Lacroix, Paris 20th.
Metro Belleville.
Tel: +33 (0)1 43 66 83 74.

**Enjoy a Phad Thai
just like in Bangkok**
Le Sukhothai
12 rue du Père Guérin, Paris 13th.
Metro Place d'Italie.
Tel: +33 (0)1 45 81 55 88.

Eat as the Vietnamese do
Le Bambou
70 rue Beaudricourt, Paris 13th.
Metro Tolbiac.
Tel: +33 (0)1 45 70 00 44.

Lose it for a noodle dish
Hokkaido
14 rue Chabanais, Paris 2nd.
Metro Pyramides.
Tel: +33 (0)1 42 60 50 95.

Single

First rendez-vous

Second rendez-vous

Wild night

Have your panties delivered

Every time the postman rings, you blush. Either you're smitten by the uniform, or you're awaiting a very special delivery. Something truly intimate. Naughty even. Something with satin and lace...

The Canadian website Panty by Post is offering a subscription that has girls feel so good that it should be reimbursed by National Health Care. It sends you a unique panty by mail every month. You can either order one at a time or subscribe for a whole year. Select your size, pay, and be on the lookout for the postman. You know how shopping for lingerie can get you high, so you can just imagine what opening such a package and discovering your underwear will do to you—those cute bows, sexy shapes, and delicate embroideries. Your own private surprise panty every month!

www.pantybypost.com
Subscription for a monthly surprise panty:
Can$ 16 (€12) for one order;
Can$ 240 (€177) for a monthly surprise for one year.
Additional cost for delivery to France.

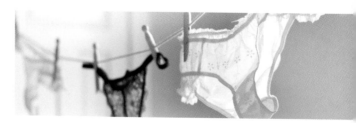

"One should always
be a little improbable."

Oscar Wilde

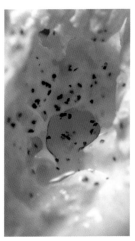

Lose your mind over an Italian cheese

Kanako

She has the softest skin, a tender body and a milky complexion.

Her sensual shapes and Italian origins make her the center of attention at every dinner party. La Burrata. It's not the name of a famous Sicilian diva. It's an Italian cheese made from cow's milk that looks just like mozzarella on the outside but hides surprising wonders on the inside.

This could be intense. After having undressed La Burrata from its green envelop, plunge your spoon into its flesh and discover the delights of a velvety, delicate cream. A touch of salt and pepper, a drop of olive oil and there you are. Pure heaven.

How can we ever thank you, Italy?

Coopérativa Latte Cisternino
- 46 rue du Faubourg Poissonnière, 10th. Metro Bonne Nouvelle.
Tel: +33 (0)1 47 70 30 36.
- 108 rue Saint-Maur, 11th. Metro Parmentier.
Tel: +33 (0)1 43 38 54 54.
- 17 rue Geoffroy St Hilaire, 5th. Metro Censier–Daubenton.
- 37 rue Godot de Mauroy, 9th. Metro Havre–Caumartin.
Open Tuesday to Saturday 10am to 1.30pm and 4.30pm to 8pm.
Fresh delivery from Campania on Thursday.
Closed Sunday and Monday.

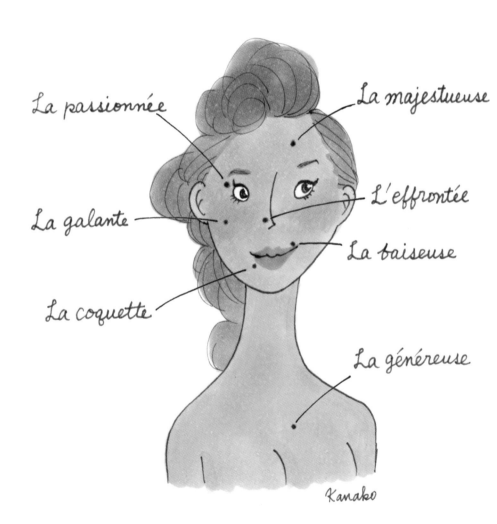

FATALE

Try the killer secret detail

On Monday, he saw the passionate woman in you. On Tuesday, he discovered you were sassy. On Wednesday, he was amazed at your generosity. On Thursday he was lost: who is she? If he only new your little secret.

A tiny flirtatious beauty mark brushes against your lip. Another peacefully rests at the corner of your eye. If you weren't born with Cindy Crawford's nevus, don't panic. Steal the secret of the 18th century courtesans and get a "mouche," a little piece of taffeta, which they used to put on their skin to enhance the paleness of their complexion and spark up their face and cleavage. But make sure you don't sow these beauty spots randomly. You must carefully place them according to the centennial rules that have proven to be the most effective in the science of seducing courtiers.

Choose your "mouche"
La passionnée ("the passionate") sets your eyes on fire. *L'effrontée* ("the impudent") is perched on your nose. *La baiseuse* (the "lover") languishes on your lips. The "coquette" hides at the corner of your mouth. *La galante* (the "gallant") rests in the middle of your cheek. *La majestueuse* (the "majestic") reigns over your forehead and *la généreuse* (the "generous") enhances your bust.

Join in on the Dead Poet's Society

Knock knock. Behind the peephole in the heavy wooden door, an eye appears and a whispering voice asks us to be patient: we're not allowed to interrupt a reading of Rimbaud! Once the sacrilege has been avoided, we are welcomed into the Poets' Club.

It is located in a small tavern created in 1961 by poet Jean-Pierre Rosnay and his muse, Tsou. It feels like home, probably because it is home to the founder's son and his family. Once seated at a table, we order drinks. It's 10pm, and all is silent. We are entering the land of poetry. One at a time, actors, singers and writers rise from their chair and recite a poem. Anybody, including you, can join in the reading, but you have to know your text by heart.

Around midnight, the evening comes to an end. Baudelaire has invited us to travel, Aragon has worshiped Elsa's eyes. You might not have hopped on a table, but you're in on a well-kept secret: the Dead Poet's Society is still alive.

Le Club des Poètes (Poets' Club)
30 rue de Bourgogne, Paris 7th.
Metro Varenne.
Poetic Soirées on Tuesday, Friday and Saturday at 10 pm.
Entrance €5, reservation required, call +33 (0)1 47 05 06 03.

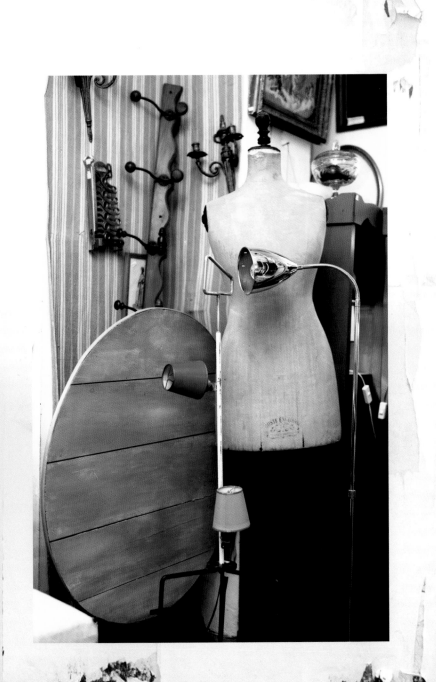

Rummage around for deco objects

You've just moved in. You've thought the place through, measured every corner. You've studied catalogues and selected your new furniture. The color of the walls seems right and the rug is well aligned. Funny how something is missing in this perfect decor.

Ikéa, Roche-Bobois, Habitat: whichever chapel you worship at, you'd better avoid the uniform look or you might lose your home's soul. Salvation is around the corner, at the flea market. Nothing compares to hunting for those precious secondhand items that will individualize your interior. Head for *les puces*, the ultimate Parisian flea market, where you can browse through the antique stands and second-hand shops. Loose yourself in a maze of unusual, charming articles. Take your time, feel, compare, cogitate, and then go ahead and bargain when you fall head over heels over an object. Amen!

Puces de Vanves (Vanves Flea market)
Along avenue Marc Sangnier
and avenue Georges Lafenestre, Paris 14th.
Saturday and Sunday 7am to 1pm.

Brocantes de Popincourt
Shops on rue du Marché Popincourt,
rue Neuve Popincourt and rue Ternaux, Paris 11th.
Metro Oberkampf or Parmentier.
Closed Monday.

"Et puis c'est tout !" ('50s to '70s shop)
72 rue des Martyrs, Paris 9th.
Metro Pigalle.
Tel: +33 (0)1 40 23 94 02.
Open Monday 2pm to 7pm and Tuesday to Saturday noon to 7.30pm.

Invent your next job

Which of these careers really exists in Paris

(answers at the bottom of the page)

Professional party-crasher
He attends your party and pretends he's having the time of his life, to liven things up.

Town crier
He collects messages and ads from the neighbors and shouts them out on the public square.

Personal lighting engineer
He follows you everywhere and makes sure you're always in the spotlight. And if you're ever overshadowed by someone, he puts the flash back on you.

Party detective
He manages to find out about secret Parisian parties and gets you invited.

Ego Booster
He writes nice comments on your Facebook pictures and calls to cheer you up on Sunday night.

Personal musician
He accompanies every moment of your life with the right music, just like in a musical.

Taster
She tastes everything before you do, to make sure it suits you: restaurants, trips, and boyfriends.

Professional heartbreaker
He's called in to break up unhappy couples.

Olivier

Town crier

2 rue Crillon, 4th

TASTER

17, PASSAGE DUBUFFET
PARIS 12TH
06 32 45 75 12 32

VALÉRIE
MAJOREL

RENÉ DELAPORTE

PERSONAL MUSICIAN

34 SQUARE DIAPASON, 19TH

TEL : 01 45 89 34 653

BENJAMIN D.

PARTY DETECTIVE

56, RUE POTAIN, PARIS 19TH

www.detectivedesoiree.com

PARC DE BAGATELLE, 16TH
TEL. 00 33 1 67 23 09 345

ALEX LIPPI

PROFESSIONAL HEARTBREAKER

MARTIN AMBLARD
PROFESSIONAL PARTY-CRASHER

PORTE DE LA MUETTE
CONTACT@ETIENNEDISCUTE.COM

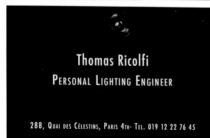

Thomas Ricolfi
PERSONAL LIGHTING ENGINEER

288, QUAI DES CÉLESTINS, PARIS 4TH- TEL. 019 12 22 76 45

EGO BOOSTER

ROMUALD POULET
10, CITE BIENAIMÉ, PARIS 18TH
WWW.BOOSTEUR-D-EGO.NET

WEAR A HAT
THAT'S MADE JUST FOR YOU

Surely you are wondering what type of hat to wear to your upcoming ultra-chic wedding at the Crillon or the Prix de Diane Derby in Chantilly. Will it be Bogart's fedora, Romy Schneider's straw hat, Jackie O's pillbox, or maybe Audrey Hepburn's feathery bibi?

Cerise is the woman you need. This young stylist welcomes you into her beautiful boutique, which also hosts her studio where she can help you whip up the ingredients to create your own unique hat.

Choose an inspiration, the 1920s,'40s or '60s... and select your material, ribbon and colors.

Be careful, you could just be mistaken for an icon.

Kanako

La Cerise sur le chapeau
11 rue Cassette, Paris 6th.
Metro Rennes.
Tel: +33 (0)1 45 49 90 53.
Open Tuesday to Saturday 1pm to 7pm.
Prices range from €70 to €140.

Prescription
for getting over your ex in Paris

MY LITTLE PARIS

—

MÉDECINE GÉNÉRALE

—

92 1 18789 4

—

Consultations :
ndi, Mardi, Mercredi, Jeudi, Vendredi
9 h - 13 h et 15 h- 20 h
Samedi 9 h - 13 h

57, rue du Prés
92300 LEVALL
Tél. : 01 47
Fax : 01 47

Diagnosis: a benign breakup

Treatment: 3 months plus follow-up if the symptoms last.

√ Stop by the Louvre everyday to admire the statue of Casanova and remind yourself of your ex boyfriend's imperfections.
Dosage: once a week for a month, then once a month.

√ Sell your ex on ebay and finally know his real value.
Dosage: once a week for a month.

√ Get a new haircut with the "Breakup special" *at the Zazen salon (38 rue du Roi de Sicile, 4th). Dosage: once at the beginning of the treatment.*

√ Call the Ego-Booster (see page 87).

d'une association agréée, les règlements par chèque sont acceptés.

d'urgence, appelez le 15.

93

"A career is wonderful,
but you can't curl up with it
on a cold night."

Marylin Monroe

Learn
Dirty Dancing

Officially? Once. Honestly? 14 times. You've seen *Dirty Dancing* so many times you know every second of the movie by heart. Now you're ready to come clean and fulfill your fantasy: learn how to dance like in *Dirty Dancing*. And... action!

Nicolas and Anne are not your typical dance teachers. They give private Dirty Dancing lessons to future brides and grooms who want to stir up the dance floor on their wedding day. Or to anyone wanting to get the swing of it for fun. A few hours of class are enough to master every step of the famous last scene. All you need is a nice white dress and pretty heels. And a partner who dares to walk in Patrick Swayze's shoes. We guarantee you'll have the time of your life.

Kanako

Dirty Dancing class
To sign up for a class, call Anne:+33 (0)6 63 91 88 82 or Nicolas: +33 (0)6 63 93 50 06) or send them an email at pouge-pouge@hotmail.fr
Classes Monday to Thursday 2pm to 5pm and on Friday night. Weekend sessions.
Price for a one-hour private class with both teachers: €100 per couple

Sip a cocktail in a dreamy hideaway

Parisians are (for once) unanimous. This place is the ultimate Paris escape. It is really really private. Located at the top of a secret stairway in the heart of Montmartre, the Hotel Particulier is an authentic villa surrounded by a lush garden, which previously belonged to the Hermès family. The villa has its own very private bar, the "Très Particulier," where reservations are absolutely mandatory. A piano, a few random tables where patrons play chess under the candlesticks, and behind the soft leather bar, there's David, the New York bartender. He's the authentic cocktail artist, who makes old and forgotten drinks come back to life before your mellow eyes. The villa also offers 5 beautiful suites, all designed by contemporary artists. Dreamy.

Bar privé Le Très Particulier
At the Hôtel Particulier de Montmartre
23 avenue Junot, Paris 18th.
Metro Blanche or Lamarck–Caulaincourt
Tel: +33 (0)1 53 41 81 40
http://hotel-particulier-montmartre.com
(Ring the bell on the black gate
and explain you're here to have a drink).
Open Wednesday to Saturday 5pm to 11pm.
Reservations required.

Have a cocktail named after you

You might find Tristan too dry or Pierre a bit chilled but Olivier might be perfect for you. The latest Parisian chic? Give your name to a cocktail created to your taste by the best bartender in the city. For once, you can be narcissistic.

Head down the Rue Dauphine to the Pixel Bar. List your favorite ingredients and Michel, the bartender, will shake your dream potion. Caramel vodka, fresh ginger, Cointreau, apricot brandy—indulge your every whim. If you like the cocktail, Michel names it after you and puts it up on the menu. If it's not right, Michel adds his special touch to make it perfect.

And last but not least, you should taste the exquisite mojito, which is officially the best in Paris.

Pixel Bar
10 rue Dauphine, Paris 6th.
Metro Odéon.
Tel: +33 (0)1 44 07 02 15 / +33 (0)6 58 41 61 15.
Open Tuesday to Saturday 5pm to 2am.

Forgotten veggies

Parsnip
Carrot's cousin

Rutabaga
Cabbage meets turnip

Jerusalem artichoke
Artichoke family

Butternut
Hint of butter

Dandelion
Salad's twin

Sweet dumpling
Kick of chestnut and hazelnut

Kanako

Rediscover forgotten veggies

"Can you believe what Simone served for dinner last night! Poor thing, she's completely out of it. Someone should tell her that asparagus is dépassé and that cucumber is so over."

Fashion and trends rule the veggie industry. After decades of being ignored by the public, old veggies are back in style. Moreover, they are starring in the new Spring-Summer collection at the farmer's market. Rent-control tenants squatting the bottom drawer of the fridge are being thrown out by vintage seedlings with quaint names such as parsnip, rutabaga and dandelion. To pick out the best items, we recommend the Proxibio stand at the organic market on the Boulevard Raspail.

Proxibio Stand
Organic market on the boulevard Raspail
(between numbers 68 and 74), Paris 6th.
Metro Raspail.

(Almost) Wear Couture

When Fashion Week starts, you always wonder where all the scraps of material from your favorite designer's collections end up. In some kind of velvety, precious, colorful paradise is your best guess. Well think again.

Eva Zingoni, a former trend-spotter for Li Edelkort and personal stylist for the rich and famous at Balenciaga, collects the leftover material from the greatest fashion designers and brings it back to her studio. Silk crêpe, printed chiffon, taffeta and metallic wool are gathered in the small apartment, waiting for their second life. We're not talking of the land of virtual fantasy here. The lady has a vision as she delicately unfolds her soft treasures and transforms them into sexy, easy to wear, modern little dresses.

Each piece is a very limited edition. Haute Couture meets Zingoni's talent. And as you try on the dream dress in her studio, Eva adjusts it to make it just right for you. It is almost too couture to be true.

Eva Zingoni
Studio: 83, allée Darius Milhaud, Paris 19th.
Metro: Ourcq or Danube.
Tel: +33 (0)1 42 49 05 32.
www.evazingoni.com
Dresses from €95 to €550.

500 NECKLACES

Don't drink and email

3.16am. You come home tipsy. After an awesome party and one too many drinks, you feel like the queen of the world and everything seems possible. You decide to check your email before going to bed. Dreadful mistake. Suddenly, out of the blue, you send a message to your long-lost ex, begging him to take you back. Then you resolve to come clean with your best friend about that bad joke in March 1998. And finally you tell your coworker what a jerk you think he is.

11.32am. You wake up aghast as your head clears and you realize what you did.

We've all been there, bitterly regretting a late-night message, which seemed so brilliant and convincing at the time, but just so cruelly pathetic the morning after. To make sure you avoid any future irreparable mistakes, Google has its own drunkometer. If you're a Gmail user, you can set the after-party option in their settings. This forbids you from sending an email before having resolved 5 simple mathematical equations in less than 60 seconds. If you fail the test, better wait till morning to send your email.

Stay on the ball though. They haven't invented a solution for text messages yet.

Available on any Gmail accounts
with English settings:
https://www.google.com/accounts/ManageAccount

PUT YOURSELf
iN Good HANds

You walk in, uptight and feeling down. You walk out, lighthearted and relaxed. Xin-Sheng is a traditional Chinese massage joint, located on the corner of "peace of mind" and really affordable. €35 for a whole hour, €20 a half-hour. Who's ever topped that in this city?

You needn't wait long after you walk in to start feeling better. The Chinese decor, the greeting from two canaries and your hosts' delicate courtesy have the immediate effect of lifting a weight off your soon-to-be-rubbed shoulders. The rest is pure delight. Choose your oil, close your eyes and enjoy. In the expert hands of the masseuse, you slowly let go of your bad day and you recover feeling in every part of your body. Hard to believe that this kind of sensory plaesure is available every day of the week, from dust till dawn...

Institut Xin-Sheng
56, rue du Faubourg Poissonnière, Paris 10th.
Metro Poissonnière or Bonne Nouvelle.
Tel: +33 (0)1 42 46 10 62.
Open daily 10am to 10pm.
Chinese massage 1hr: €35 (body).
Thai massage 1hr: €40 (body).
Back or head massage ½ hr: €20.
Foot massage 1hr: €30.

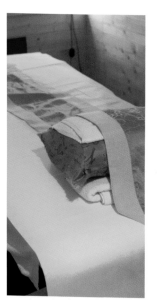

Accept
a non-marriage proposal

"Mademoiselle Pinceau, will you agree not to marry Monsieur Martin?" Did the mayor just put his foot in it? Not at all. On this particular Sunday, you're welcome to say no!

Every year, during the Montmartre Grape Harvest Festival, Parisian couples gather on the Place des Abbesses, before the wall dedicated to love. They patiently wait in line to be non-married by Daniel Vaillant, the mayor of the 18th arrondissement. This ceremony gives these *amoureux*, reluctant to take traditional vows, an opportunity to express their love in public. As for the non-non-marrying kind, you are invited to enjoy the party, taste the local Montmartre wine (*cuvée des vignes de la Butte*), browse the arty streets and attend the many dances held on the hills of Montmartre.

Non-wedding ceremony
Place des Abbesses, during the Montmartre Grape Harvest Festival, every year in October.
All information on
www.fetedesvendangesdemontmartre.com
Couples can sign in at the 18th arrondissement town hall or by phone: +33 (0)1 53 41 17 82.

Kanako

"You can find inspiration in anything, and if you can't… look again."

Comforting blank page
(Unload all your troubles on this wall)

Kanako

Turn your kids into little Picassos

Your youngest child draws like a god. And you've been bragging to everyone that he is no less than a future Picasso. His choice of colors is amazing, and his subjects are dramatically insightful. It's time you helped him express himself fully.

Send his latest Crayola drawing to the e-glue website and they will print the masterpiece on a giant sticker. There is a good chance your living room will shortly be transformed into a gallery. And now everyone will appreciate his masterpieces.

From €39 to €139.
Shipments are worldwide.
www.e-glue.fr

CATCH A CONCERT IN 7TH HEAVEN

"Rendezvous tomorrow in 7th heaven"
If you happen to be the lucky gal to receive this text message, answer on the spot. You don't want to miss this memorable evening: a private concert on the terrace of an apartment overlooking Montmartre. Are you in?

When Damien and Julie settled in their apartment with a plunging view over the Sacré Cœur, they decided they had to share their good fortune with others. So, on summer evenings, they round up perfect strangers and welcome them into their home for an open-air concert. About 30 people, invited at the last minute by means of a text message, gather on the terrace and listen to music from 7th heaven. You might be next.

Les Concerts du 7ᵉ ciel
More information on the website: http://7ciel.net/concerts/
To win an invitation for the next concert,
take part in the Pop News contest.

© Guillaume Sautereau/POPnews.com

Indulge
in the best ham in the world

Fruity, feminine, supple, fragrant, powerful, complex. Are we talking about wine? No, but tasting this can evoke similar heights of infinite pleasure and once you start, there's no stopping. It's Bellota Bellota. It's simply the best ham in the world.

Its tender texture melts in your mouth like caramel, caresses your palette, and teases your taste buds with its range of marbled flavors.

It's served in a volcano-shaped dish placed over a candle-warmed hot plate so the petals of ham are slightly warmed and shiny. You're only allowed to use your fingers! Complete your meal with some exquisite tapas and a smoky Spanish wine and you'll experience the perfect gastronomical trinity.

Jabugo Iberico & Co
11, rue Clément Marot, Paris 8th.
Metro Franklin D. Roosevelt.
Tel: +33 (0)1 47 20 03 13.
Open Monday to Saturday 10am to 9pm (8pm on Saturday).

Bellota Bellota
18 rue Jean Nicot, Paris 7th.
Metro La-Tour-Maubourg.
Tel: +33 (0)1 53 59 96 96.
Open Tuesday to Saturday noon to 3pm and 7pm to 11pm.
www.bellota-bellota.com

Dress
like a VIP

Stylish girls know the trick. They'll never take "outfit" for an answer to any fashion question. They mix and match, Chanel with H&M... and even better, they add vintage.

Vintage? The mere idea of rummaging through piles of smelly old clothes has you running straight to Gap.

Why not run instead to Sylvie Chateigner's boutique for a VIP coaching session? Not only does Sylvie master the art of vintage, but she also selects clothes and accessories as she would guests at the most exclusively hip Parisian party. Check it out: a sharp selection of luxury vintage clothes (YSL, Alaia, Dior, etc.) located on the main floor of her shop in the République neighborhood, and lots of affordable pieces in the basement (short silk dress €10, military style tunic €14, etc.).

What can I say? You may now consider yourself a V.I.P!

Thanx God I'm a V.I.P.
12, rue de Lancry, Paris 10th.
Metro Jacques Bonsergent or République.
Open Tuesday to Sunday, 2pm to 10pm.

ZEN

The feel-good pause

Instead of gulping this book straight down, why don't you sip it one idea at a time. Go get the mail, make yourself a cup of tea, cut that annoying loose thread hanging from your dress—or hop into this yoga position.

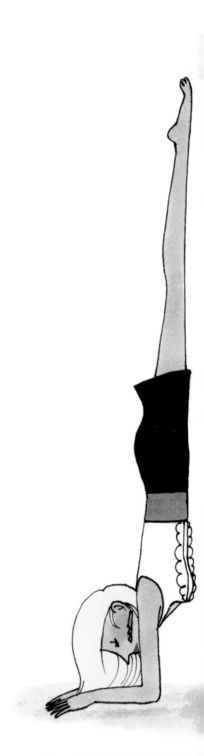

Make a deal with the granny gang

It's freezing outside. Wouldn't it be nice if you had a nice grandma to warm up your frostbitten ears? Jérémy Emsellem, founder of Golden Hook website, has recruited a group of serial-knitting grandmothers to provide homemade hats and trendy scarves to heat chilly fashionistas all over the world.

If you want to meet the gang, browse the Golden Hook website. Start by choosing your granny: it could be Sarah, 85 years old and fan of the Wheel of Fortune; Maïté, polka dancer; or Ginette, gossip-knitter. Then select the design of your hat or scarf, its shape, material and color. Would you rather wear a classic red bob, an angora Peruvian or a yellow cashmere scarf? The final touch: the name of your granny, engraved on a small label inside. Don't forget to say thank you!

Order your hats and scarves on Golden Hook
http://www.goldenhook.fr/
Hat: from €50 to €70.
Scarf: €90.

125

Brunch to the tune of the four seasons

Spring

Peacefully settled on a pastoral terrace in the shadow of leafy trees, you let those sweet and savory flavors mix gently on your plate. Relish all-you-can-eat scrambled eggs, chocolate delicacies, smoked salmon, freshly squeezed juices, *pains au chocolat*, and croissants.

L'Entrepôt
7/9 rue Francis de Pressensé, Paris 14th.
Metro Pernety. Tel: +33 (0)1 47 40 07 50.
€25 for brunch, reservations recommended.

Fall

Find a plump cushion to nestle into, and once you're as cozy as a hen in a coop, pick out your favorite egg recipe from a menu of more than 100 and jazz it up by adding a selected glamorous ingredient: truffle, beaufort cheese, asparagus, foie gras, salmon or even a touch of lavender. Brunch for egg lovers.

Eggs & Co
11, rue Bernard Palissy, Paris 6th.
Metro Saint-Germain-des-Prés.
Tel: +33 (0)1 45 44 02 52.
www.eggsandco.fr
Reservations highly recommended.
Brunch served Wednesday to Sunday (€22).
Open Wednesday, Thursday and Friday
noon to 2pm and 7.30pm to 10.30pm.
Open Saturday and Sunday noon to 4.30pm.

Summer

Enjoy a morning of pure Provence nonchalance; the only detail missing is the cicada. Have your brunch under the centennial olive trees in the hall or on the charming rooftop terrace with its luscious greenery and typical blue shutters. Feels like a little loft in a valley somewhere in the South of France.

La Bellevilloise
19-21, rue Boyer, Paris 20th.
Metro Menilmontant or Gambetta.
Tel: +33 (0)1 46 36 07 07.
www.labellevilloise.com

Winter

The cold is gripping and the nights are glacial. You could use a friendly brunch to warm up your spirits. The ambiance at Depur is that of an old British club; it makes you want to cuddle up in a cashmere blanket and daydream—just like at home.

DEPUR
4 bis rue Saint-Sauveur, Paris 2nd.
Tel: +33 (0)1 40 26 69 66.
Metro Réaumur–Sébastopol.
Open Monday to Saturday 8am to 2am
and Sunday 11am to 4pm (brunch costs €28).
Reservations required.

Turn your Home into a (coffee-table) book

After years of looking for the right one, you've finally settled into that apartment. You've committed yourself to making it beautiful, by spending hours at flea markets, improving it down to the tiniest detail and repairing anything broken. But then someday, inevitably, you break up. You want a bigger place. More space, more light.

Sure, you're happy to move on, but there is no way you are leaving all these happy memories behind. Photographer Ricardo Bloch's got it. It takes him but a few weeks and he'll shoot each corner of your place and wrap it all up into a unique coffee-table book called *Lifescape*. A place to remember.

www. ricardobloch.com
Tel: +33 (0)6 67 75 97 79.
Price on request.
Contact: contact@ricardobloch.com

"Life is like riding a bicycle. To keep your balance you must keep moving."

Einstein

Examples
of recent cases:

Are women more beautiful in
the summertime?

Can we light back the stars?

To love a little is to love too much?

Do good things always have to come
to an end?

Should we burn our love letters?

Should we grow up?

Do we have to finish our plates?

Can we heal from all words?

Is tomorrow another day?

Is the copy better than the original?

Should we love crazy people?

Is it possible to exist without living?

Are women good guys?

Are black cats unhappy?

Attend
a crazy trial

Subject 'du jour'
Is tomorrow another day?

Hanako

Just imagine. A handsome young lawyer is getting ready to stand up and plead a case. You expect drama, emotions, tears. There he goes. "Ladies and gentlemen of the jury, I am here today to defend the opinion that a woman's right to Manolo Blahnik stilettos should be written in the Constitution."

You are not dreaming. You are attending the Eloquence Competition organized by the Paris Bar, where the best Parisian orators confront each other with powerful words on the most disconcerting subjects. Vibrant pleas and unexpected arguments are brandished to win over and convince the audience of the rightness of their cause. Should we burn love letters? Is it safe to cry on the third date?

Law and disorder is more fun.

Information on coming dates: ***www.laconference.net***
Library of the Paris Court.
Boulevard du Palais, Paris 4 th.
Metro Saint-Michel.

Make a stop at the chignon bar

Natalie Portman wears hers à la ballerina, Audrey Hepburn invented the banana, while Diane Kruger likes her braids. There's a bun style to every woman. Yours? A quick twist held together by an old headband. Needless to say you're in dire need of a stop at the chignon bar.

In an 18th century mansion, Marianne Gray's hair salon features a special "counter." Behind it, your hair is expertly gathered, pulled, wrapped, backcombed, twisted and pinned, according to your wishes. All that happens in two ticks, and without spending a fortune. Remember that a bun perched on top of a head gives as much allure as a pair of stilettos.

Chignon Bar at Marianne Gray's Hair Salon
52, rue Saint-André-des-Arts, Paris 6th.
To book an appointment, call: +33 (0)1 46 33 72 32.
Prices vary according to the time necessary to make the bun:
€20 for 10 minutes, €40 for 20 minutes etc.

Attend
a clandestine dinner

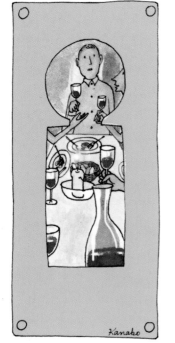

You don't know the address, or the menu, nor have you ever met the other guests. What you do know is that the evening should be fascinating and the meal exquisite. The underground dinner is an American concept, directly imported to Parisian apartments. The idea is to mingle with a dozen strangers over a gourmet dinner.

Our favorite is *Hidden Kitchen*. A young American couple, passionate about food, welcomes you into their Parisian home and treats you to a gastronomic meal. No less than ten dishes and subtle wines, perfectly matched to the meal, parade on the table, each solemnly announced like in a four-star restaurant. Little by little, the crowd loosens up, conversations open up, and acquaintances are made: a lot of Americans, a couple from Boston, a New York architect and also a few Parisians, trying out their English.

If the idea of an underground dinner with complete strangers is irresistible to you, write to hkreservations@gmail.com and wait for further instructions. Be patient, you might need to wait a few weeks to unveil the mysteries of the *Hidden Kitchen*.

Hidden Kitchen
hkmenus.com/french.htm
Reservation by mail to hkreservations@gmail.com
Price: €80 per guest.

SPICY

SET UP YOUR OWN adulterous MOMENT

HOW TO TRANSFORM YOUR PARTNER INTO YOUR SECRET LOVER

1. Book a room in a hotel by the hour, in a distant neighborhood.

2. Dress in leather.

3. Send your partner a mysterious and sensual message, offering a rendezvous.

4. Find a no-fail reason so that your boss lets you escape for a few hours.

5. Arrive first.

6. Refrain from saying "Hi honey!" when he enters the room.

7. After an hour, leave the room discreetly while he's still asleep, intentionally forgetting your fragranced silk scarf on the bed.

8. When you meet back home later that night, act as if nothing happened and never ever mention this stolen moment.

Fight
the Sunday night blues

You never see it coming. You hit the Paris scene with friends on Saturday, you laze around in bed on Sunday and then, when night falls, it shows up, almost unexpectedly: the Sunday night blues.

The very insightful owners of *La Famille*, a restaurant in Montmartre, have found the perfect remedy to warm your spirits and your taste buds. Every first Sunday of the month, they offer haven to endangered weekenders in the form of a Special Discount Menu combined with some much needed socializing. For €10, you'll be served a 3-course creative meal (such as Saint-Moret cheese and basil soup, Japanese mushroom pasta and cosmopolitan crumble) and nice conversation with your new Sunday night companions. Doors open at 8pm, so better get there a little early, or much later.

Sunday night special at La Famille
41 rue des Trois Frères, Paris 18th.
Tel: +33 (0)1 42 52 11 12.
Metro Abbesses.
Super Discount menu for €10 (appetizer-main course-desert)
every first Sunday of the month, from 8pm (be there at 7.45pm).
Reservations impossible.

Have fresh produce delivered to your home

Whenever the bad weather prevents you from wearing your little polka-dot dress and your cute basket to shop for fresh produce at the open-air market, Monsieur Fraicolo does it for you.

He not only shops for you, he takes your shopping list and goes all the way to legendary Rungis, the huge market which supplies the entire city of Paris. There, he selects the best quality for a much lower price: organic vegetables, the juiciest seasonal fruit, fresh and tender meat, hams and pâtés, and fresh roses straight from Africa.

He bargains fiercely with the traders, making his way from market to market, to fill your basket. Once he's done shopping, he hops back on his eco-friendly bike and delivers your produce to your home or even your office, as you like. Monsieur Fraicolo is truly an exceptional gentleman.

www.fraicolo.fr
Minimum basket: €39.
Delivery cost: €5.99 in Paris and the suburbs.

Kanako

LAUGH OUT loud

Kanako

Have you heard the latest joke in the city? It goes like this: "It's about a photographer guy who invites anonymous or famous people into his studio every day to take their picture..." and it ends up with a shot of them laughing out loud! Whatever happens during the 15-minute rendezvous to generate this hilarity is a total mystery.

The LOL project by David Ken collects portraits of very merry Parisians in their most beautiful, natural poses. David shoots people for free in his studio and feeds an online gallery. The studio is open to anybody. Young, old, worried, relaxed, in a hurry, up, down, chic or casual. David has 15 minutes to make them laugh their heart out. The idea is full of disarming kindness. He has a dream. Make Paris smile.

Be part of the LOL project

If you want to spend 15 minutes of pure happiness and have a pretty incredible photo of yourself, sign up on http://www.lolproject.com/inscription/
www.lolproject.com

Change your lingerie, change your life

You worry about your figure. But do you really think your breasts can blossom in this tiny bra? And your buttocks, can they really feel comfortable spilling out from a thong? Maybe your cute round belly is fed up with being squeezed into a shorty.

Before contemplating surgery, you might want to consider changing your lingerie. At least, that's what Laetitia Schlumberger strongly believes. As a genuine corset maker, she sees grace where you only see inches or fat, and she has a way of beautifying even the most unloved silhouette.

Two hours are enough for Laetitia to storm through your lingerie drawer and advise you on the shapes and fabrics of underwear which can accentuate, reshape, soften, conceal and remodel the assets that Mother Nature has given you. If you need her to, she takes you to the store herself and helps you concoct your ideal lingerie collection.

Contact Laetitia Schlumberger by phone: +33 (0)6 20 52 49 66.
www.malingeriemerendbelle.com
For a 2-hour session at your home: €160.
For a 4-hour session at your home and shopping: €300.

Take the pencil test

How firm are your breasts? To answer, we dare you to take this test, just like our grandmothers used to. With your bust naked, position a pencil just under your breasts.

Kanako

A/ If the pencil falls, you're perfect.
B/ If the pencil's stuck, too bad (purchase a strong maintenance bra and, to make you feel better, think of all the divine breasts that have failed this test for decades.)

Have lunch at the Market

Can you live in an international city and still find yourself walking around a village market? *Bien sûr, c'est Paris !*

If you're strolling on the busy Rue de Bretagne in the upper Marais, stop for lunch or grocery shopping at the Marché des Enfants Rouges, named after the red uniform worn by the children who used to live in the former orphanage located here.

Lively voices of sellers echo throughout this covered, 17th-century market, hailing bypassers to bask in the scent of their fresh flowers, or even taste their wine or regional French produce. Foie gras, fine cheese and Bordeaux wine mix with delicious couscous, delicate sushi and Italian dishes. Pick your favorites from these fresh and colorful foods and enjoy your lunch!

Paris does seem like a village sometimes.

Marché des enfants rouges
Open Tuesday to Saturday 8.30am to 1pm and 4pm to 7.30pm;
Sunday 8.30am to 2pm.
39 rue de Bretagne, Paris 3rd.
Metro Arts et Métiers.

Kanako

Your Top 10 for this year:

1. Top encounter
....

2. Best lesson learnt
....

3. Party of the year
....

4. Unforgettable text message
....

5. Best outfit
....

6. Most shameful moment
....

7. Most shattering words
....

8. Most overwhelming orgasm
....

9. A small step
....

10. A big step
....

INDEX

Small Pleasures

Unusual

Culture

Bonus

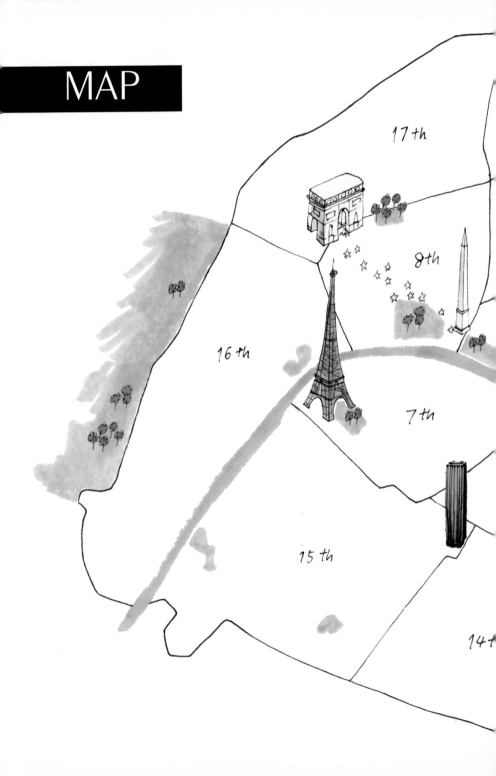

MAP

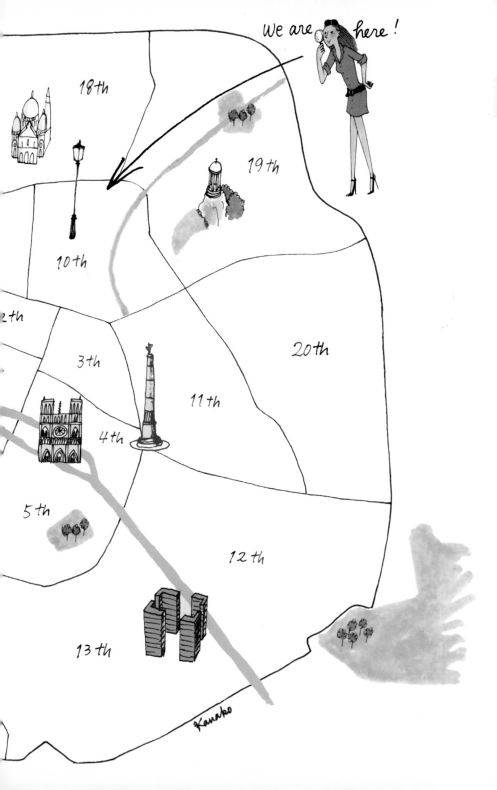

Merci:

Merci, Paris, which inspires us every morning.
Merci, metro line 4, which gives us a boost when we run out of inspiration.
Merci, Cédric and his olives, for having been our first find.
Merci, "forward" key, for having enabled My Little Paris to grow so fast.
Merci, Toni, for helping us share our secrets worldwide.
Merci, our publisher, for having accepted all of our preposterous ideas.
Merci, Catherine and Mademoiselle Lilly, for nourishing our little world.
Merci, Amandine for all the emotions she unleashes with her pen.
Merci, Anne-Flore, for helping us make our ideas grow and come to life.
Merci, Céline, our engine.
Merci, Bruno, our rock.
Merci, Kanako, our star.
And merci, Fany, for always challenging us to spice up our lives.

But most of all, merci, our dear readers. We hope never to disappoint you.

This book was produced by:

Fany Péchiodat, founder of My Little Paris
Amandine Péchiodat, editor in chief of My Little Paris
Anne-Flore Brunet, editor in chief of My Little Paris
Catherine Taret, editor of the book, contributing editor for My Little Paris
Ana Webanck, assistant project manager
Céline Orjubin, sales manager
Mademoiselle Lilly, art director of the book. email: mademoiselilly@gmail.com
Kanako, illustrator of My Little Paris
Toni Taret, proofreader for My Little Paris in English

Éditions du Chêne, in charge of the project:
Publisher: Volcy Loustau
Art Director: Nancy Dorking
Proofreading: Charlotte Monnier
Production: Amandine Sevestre
Revision: Jeanne Cheynel

PHOTO CREDITS
© Florent Drillon: p. 6-7/14/30-31/42/48/50-51/60/71/78/82/84/87-88/
101/103/107/117/128/134/141/144. www.florentdrillon.com
© Mairie de Paris: p. 31; © Matthias Biberon: p. 40; ©Anne-Laure Jacquart: p. 47; © Baudouin: p.6
©Adam Rootman: p.75; ©Antoine Ricardou: p. 91; ©Emilien Cancet: p.108; © HYPERLINK
"http://www.e-eglue.fr"
www.e-eglue.fr: p.115; © Depur: p.127; © Charlotte Lascève: p. 130-131; © Tedx: p.147;

IMAGE AND PHOTO STYLING
Elodie Rambaud : p. 30-31/58/78/101/128/144. http://elodierambaud.com/